A QUESTION OF IDENTITY

Charles August Schwabe

A QUESTION OF IDENTITY

The extraordinary exploits of a Sussex
family from Munich to the Somme,
St. Petersburg and the Hollywood Hills

TIM PARKER

COUNTRY BOOKS

Published by Country Books
Courtyard Cottage, Little Longstone, Bakewell, Derbyshire DE45 1NN
Tel: 01629 640670
e-mail: dickrichardson@country-books.co.uk
www.countrybooks.biz
www.sussexbooks.co.uk

ISBN 978-1-910489-48-2

British Library Cataloguing in Publication Data.
A catalogue record for this book is available from the British Library.

To John

With my very best wish

CONTENTS

Thm Parker,
Jny 2018

ACKNOWLEDGEMENTS

First and foremost this book would never have been written without the help and enthusiasm of Kathryn Whyte, who found us and told us who we were. Kathryn for her part received much help from Ian Sage from the Parker side of the family, as did I. He painstakingly uncovered much of our story. Then there is Julian, what would I have done without him, and my daughter Donna who has lived with the Schwabes for some four years. I thank her from the bottom of my heart. There are many others who have helped in so many ways: John Wallbank for his meticulous research, my grandson Niki for his contribution, Hope Delicta, Rosemary Konecki, Stephen Bridges, Roger Clifton Moore, William Catchpole and James Parker. While I am credited as being the author, without the family's co-operation this extraordinary story would not have see the light of day. Nor can I forget our publisher, Richard Richardson, the man brave enough to take us all on.

Finally, my love and thanks to my family and as always to my wife Beth, for her love and encouragement, and for making it all possible.

Tim Parker 2018

FOREWORD

When the family asked me to write this foreword, I felt proud and privileged, but unsure how to approach it. Never-the-less, as the fifth generation of an extraordinary family, I took the challenge.

Our family story is set against the backdrop of some of the events that have shaped modern history. At once both terrible and remarkable, it follows the devastating sorrow of war to the neon lights of the Hollywood Hills.

The most famous member of my family is the screen actor Cecil Parker. But, until we started on this endeavour, none of us knew that his brother Charles Schwabe, as well as being a brilliant chemist and musician, was a British spy in Petrograd during the Russian Revolution. In addition, there's an extraordinary supporting cast of characters: Arthur Conan-Doyle, the War poet, Edmund Blunden, Arthur Ransome, Harold Macmillan and Dennis Parker, a decorated R.A.F pilot. Secrets, espionage and celebrity are the headlines, but a sensitively told account of a family that survived great hardship, while remaining proud, resilient and with their sense of humour intact, provide its substance.

My great-great grandfather Charles August Schwabe was born in Bavaria, the illegitimate son of a hunter, and from this un-compromising beginning he arrived in England in 1890, aged 30. Within a year he had married my great-great grandmother Kate Parker, a church organist, and had taken charge of the only luxury hotel in Hastings, 'The Albany'. Together they had eleven children, which wasn't unusual in those days, but what I didn't know was just how singular they and their children were. In often difficult circumstances, the Schwabe children were raised to be determined, brave, joyful, and above all, to keep going no matter what.

The First World War was without parallel the most terrible conflict the world has ever suffered. Not only was the human loss devastating, but the effect it had on the families back home would last for generations to come. The Schwabes played their part with great courage. Three of August and Kate's eldest sons fought on the front line and the family back home soldiered on even in the face of distrust and prejudice; they had a German surname.

In 1915, ill and heartbroken by the war, August died of cancer. Kate was on her own, her position desperate. With growing casualty lists and increasing anger for all things German, she changed the family name from Schwabe to Parker, telling her children who were still at home that it was to be a secret.

The war killed a generation of young men. I always knew that, but it wasn't until I learnt about the lives of my great-great aunts that I had any real sense of just what that meant. Over a million and a half women were left without the possibility of ever finding a husband. But the Schwabe sisters, although mourning the loss of their brother and fiancés, with strong minded courage carved out new paths for themselves, and lived full and cheerful lives.

While the eldest brothers were fighting for their country as front-line soldiers, the younger siblings were left at home to face a bewildering, terrifying and complicated future. They were forced to question who they were. Which leads me to the title – A Question of Identity.

My great great-grandfather August arrived in England as an immigrant, and quickly took to his adopted nation. He married an English girl and became a respected hotelier, with a family deep rooted in the English seaside town of Hastings. When the War broke out, the family name was Schwabe. Once the War had ended, it had become Parker.

Today, immigration is high on the political and social agenda. What this story highlights, and what is all too easily forgotten, is that most of us are immigrants or the descendants of immigrants. We all question our identity, but there is no doubt that our island has been enriched by both resisted conquerors and welcomed settlers, who for one reason or another have wished to make their home here. The Vikings, the Romans, the Normans, the Huguenots, the West Indians and settlers from many other lands have all done so.

As fascinating as the historical intrigue is, it isn't where the true story lies. Throughout the book there is a timeless message that will never cease to hold meaning and relevance to us all: family. It is over 125 years since Kate and August married. Their spirit of courage, love and laughter remains despite the ravages of two world wars. I'm proud to be part of our family and to introduce our remarkable story.

Nikolas Stojcevski
3 October, 2017

WHO WERE THE SCHWABES

It is some time since I began writing our family story, hesitating at first and wondering if it was the right thing to do. It has proved a more difficult task than I had ever imagined but with the help of our family a remarkable story has emerged; a story of great courage, danger, love and laughter, but also of illness, tragedy, despair and loss.

There is much to tell: How the family coped with the death of their father, Charles August Schwabe in 1915, in the middle of the Great War and the change of name to Parker, their mother Kate's maiden name, a desperate decision to try and protect the family in the dangerous and difficult years of the First World War and indeed the Second World War.

Charles August Schwabe was born in Obbach near Frankfurt in 1860. He was the son of Dorothea Schwabe. A German, but in those days Bavaria was still an independent state. In 1890 Charles arrived in England – quite why we still don't know – but within a few weeks he had fallen in love with one Kate Parker, a Church Organist from Lichfield, and bought The Albany, a luxury hotel in Hastings. August, as I like to call him, was clearly a fast mover and had money.

In November 1890 August and Kate had a grand wedding in Lichfield, a honeymoon on the Isle of Wight and then settled in Hastings to run The Albany and start a family. August and Kate's first son, Charles was born in autumn 1981, soon to be followed by the birth of a further six girls and four boys.

Three of August's eldest boys were front line soldiers in the 1914-18 War against Germany. We have their records. Many of the family had a wretched time, not only the ones that went to war. Margery Parker's fiancé was killed in the trenches and her career as a concert pianist was ended by severe arthritis, but she had courage and a splendid sense of humour.

There is no doubt that Charles August Schwabe and Kate Parker, together with their immediate family, have left a proud inheritance and an amazing story.

CHAPTER ONE
1890, CHARLES AUGUST AND KATE PARKER MARRY. THE ALBANY HOTEL

Charles August Schwabe was my grandfather. I keep his ivory paper knife on my desk, it has a silver band which holds the horn handle and the blade together. In truth it is a rather ugly implement but, over the years, it has become a treasured possession. In addition my aunt Audrey Parker, who was born a Schwabe, gave me my grandfather's signet ring shortly before she died. I wear the ring from time to time and am proud to do so and, yes, I am wearing his ring this morning as I begin to write my family's story, one of misfortune, courage, love and laughter...

We don't know exactly where Charles August Schwabe met Kate Parker for the first time, but it would have been somewhere near Hastings. Kate was born in Lichfield, Staffordshire, but when she was in her teens, her parents moved south where they joined other members of the Parker family.

'A pretty girl,' August might have said to himself on meeting Kate, 'and what an advantage that she knows her music.' Kate often played the organ in her church during Sunday Service. August knew from experience that music, food, and good service were vital ingredients in the running of a luxury hotel. In February 1890, August had become a shareholder in and the manager of The Albany, the best hotel in Hastings, and was

The Ballroom of the Albany Hotel, below Eastern Cliffs, Hastings

determined to succeed. Perhaps he thought, with a touch of cunning, that he might persuade Kate to play the piano for the Albany's tea dances; that would save a bob or two.

Kate for her part would have been equally impressed. 'Who was this energetic and beautifully dressed German, Charles August Schwabe, who managed the Albany with such panache? He could dance too, and looked remarkably handsome in his white tie and tails. A pity about the Schwabe name but did that matter? Everybody knew that most of the Royal family were German in one way or the other, and the Germans had always been more reliable than the French.'

Before long August and Kate were engaged to be married. The couple enjoyed themselves exploring Sussex with its beautiful countryside, its rivers and its castles. Hastings too was full of interest. It had been one the first seaside towns to be connected to the railway and had many attractions: good property, green open spaces, an air of optimism, and of course the sea; it even had its own pier. Most days, in the early morning, August would visit the fish market and choose the best fish for his guests. The remains of this once thriving business, together with a crumbling breakwater still nestle below Hastings Eastern Cliff.

Life in the summer of 1890 was good for Kate and August, and the wedding was fixed for 15th November. It was to be in Kate's home town of Lichfield. Kate was 19 and August 30. The two of them were very much in love, with high hopes. The wedding was a great success with the Parker family there to cheer them on. It was a splendid occasion and the weather was perfect, but it seemed that there were few if any friends from Germany.

At the end of that happy day the couple left for their honeymoon, a few days in Cheltenham and then on to The Isle of Wight, two very fashionable places where the aspiring manager of Hasting's very best hotel would want to be seen.

On returning home to the Albany, Kate and August wasted no time in starting a family and in the autumn of 1891 their first son, a fine healthy boy, Charles Parker Schwabe, was born. There was much rejoicing. Charles was soon followed by Dorothea, Marjorie, Sydney, Elsie, Cecil, Kathleen, Godfrey, Eric, Audrey, and Rosa. A talented and gregarious family – how would they fare in the difficult years that lay ahead? But that is still to

The Albany Hotel, beneath Eastern Cliffs in Hastings

come. What was their father like and what do we really know about him?

Much of the first part of Charles August's life remains a mystery. We know that he was born in Bavaria, the illegitimate son of Dorothea, his father being described as a hunter. A question that members of our family ponder from time to time is whether or not he was a Jew? The answer is finely balanced. I remember my father driving me to London one day and remarking that he would not play golf at a particular Golf Club. 'Why not?' I asked. 'They don't accept Jews,' he replied. I thought nothing of it at the time but for some strange reason I have never forgotten the conversation. But, maybe the Parker Schwabes worry too much: our grandmother or great, great grandmother, depending on when you were born, was certainly a Christian. So in the strictest sense, none of our family is Jewish and never have been.

Despite knowing so little about August's early life, we know something of his character. He had wide interests, in sport, politics and the great issues of the day. He was good company, a generous man who loved a drink and a joke. He was also a very good sportsman, a tennis player and swimmer who passed on his love of sport to his children.

As time went on there were increasing difficulties with the family budget. The boys, as soon as they were old enough, were sent to private boarding schools, and while the girls went to local schools, there were always the extras – music lessons, art classes, needle work, French lessons and expensive clothes. After much discussion it seemed that the only way out was for August to take on another job and that's exactly what he did taking over the management of The Royal Bath Hotel in Bournemouth for Sir Merton Russell-Cotes who became a friend as well as an employer, while Kate remained at the Albany doing her best to manage it.

The family was divided, some living with their mother and the others with their father, an uneasy compromise but it saved on the house-keeping. Unusually (he didn't tell me much about his childhood) my father told me something about life in the Royal

From 1884 paddle steamers went from Hastings Pier along the coast to Eastbourne and Brighton, and over the Channel to Boulogne

Bath Hotel.

"Five of us children were living with my dad at The Royal Bath Hotel in a staff flat which was above the main entrance. The other members of our family were either at the Albany or at boarding school. Sometimes my mother would come over for a few days. The routine in the evening never varied. At 6pm precisely my father would take his bath. He would then dress in full evening dress – white tie and tails – kiss such of us who were there and at 7pm, putting on a pair of long white gloves, would announce 'I must now go and greet my guests'."

Although the Albany continued to do well, times were changing. Travelling abroad was becoming cheaper and more reliable making it ever more difficult to make money from an English Seaside Luxury Hotel. Then in 1914, war broke out across Europe.

CHAPTER 2

THE WAR YEARS: KATE TAKES OVER AND THE BROTHERS SIGN UP

In the spring of 1908 Charles August Schwabe became a British Citizen. He was very proud to have been accepted. He liked the English, their way of life, their sense of fair play and love of sport. August had varied interests and loved discussing the matters of the day with his wide circle of friends. Sir Arthur Conan Doyle was a regular guest at the Albany and at The Royal Bath Hotel, and August and Conan Doyle would spend many happy hours watching cricket together. Was Godfrey, Gas to his friends, christened Godfrey Arthur Schwabe in honour of Conan Doyle? I am sure of it.

Charles August himself was no mean sportsman; he was a very good tennis player and a powerful swimmer. His love of sport extended to many of his family and the following generations. With his own family it seemed that August was something of a no-nonsense man. Teaching his children to swim, he would give them a ride on his back and then slowly submerge; it was sink or swim.

All matters considered August was very much an Englishman, albeit a German by birth. While international tensions grew, few thought that there would be war with Germany; in many ways the two countries were very close and when war was declared in 1914 August was heartbroken. 'It will be a calamity,' he told his

Sir Arthur Conan Doyle

friends. Then, no sooner had the war started, but he was visited by the Hastings Police. Would he be sent to the Isle of Man with other aliens? That didn't happen – the Police declared him a loyal subject – but their visit must have been a shock and a humiliation for a proud man.

King George V was King of England, his cousin, Wilhem II, Kaiser of Germany. Asquith was Prime Minister and Winston Churchill, First Lord of The Admiralty. In many places, much to August's disgust, the outbreak of war was greeted with cheers and enthusiasm. There were queues and brass bands playing at the recruiting offices. 'It will all be over in a year; better join up now so as not to miss the fun' was a popular opinion. But there were some sane voices, 'The lamps are going out all over Europe, we shall not see them relit in our lifetime,' said Edward Grey the Foreign Secretary. He was right. It was a ruinous war causing distress and hardship throughout the world.

It was accepted without question that those of August and Kate's sons who were old enough should join the British Army. As far as August was concerned it was their duty. The first brother to enlist, in October 1914, was August and Kate's eldest son, Charles, who had been working in the textile trade and living in Bolton for some four years. He had been awarded C&G medals for fabric

Left to right: *Lt. Charles Parker Schwabe, Public School Corps. 3rd Battalion Royal Fusiliers, City of London Regiment. Sidney Philip Schwabe, 5th Battalion Royal Sussex Regiment. Cecil Schwabe, 5th Battalion Royal Sussex Regiment.*

printing in 1908 and 1910. He was a brave, clever, talented man and something of a musician. *The London Gazette* reported on 27th October 1914 that Charles, as part of the Public Schools Battalions, had joined the Royal Fusiliers and had been appointed a Lieutenant.

After he was commissioned Charles made a short visit to the Albany dressed in his officers' uniform. It was a proud moment for August and Kate as their eldest son received congratulations on his promotion. His visit was a boost for the whole family and in particular for August, who was not well. He was losing weight and suffering from stomach cramps; something was wrong.

Next to enlist in 1914 were Sydney Schwabe and his brother Cecil Schwabe. They both joined the Royal Sussex Regiment, popularly known as Lowther's Lambs. One Colonel Claude Lowther, owner of Herstmonceaux Castle in Sussex, had received permission from the War Office to raise battalions of local men for the army. It was thought that the recruits from 'the men of Sussex' would make excellent soldiers and that it would be an advantage to keep them together. A sound idea but ultimately squandered by the incompetent leadership of the British Front Line generals.

Christmas Day lunch.
The Southdowns Royal Sussex Regiment at Hertsmonceux Castle in 1914

The English Conservative politician, Colonel Claude William Henry Lowther
1870-1921

Herstmonceux Castle, East Sussex

The two brothers were to spend the better part of 18 months training in the grounds of the oldest brick-built castle in England and one of the most unusual in the land. The training that made the Royal Sussex one of the best army volunteer units was long and hard but there was time for sport and other activities which both the brothers would have enjoyed. The picture of the brothers and others larking in their tent is a happy one. Having said that, their Christmas dinner looks like short commons. In December 1915 Sydney was promoted to Sergeant. He was a kind and thoughtful man, good at his job, had plenty of friends, and like his father, a good sportsman.

Cecil Schwabe was very different from his brother Sydney, but the two of them became inseparable. As a young man Cecil had been schooled abroad for some three years, and enjoyed a rather different education from his brothers. His mother Kate must have recognised his talent for music and the arts and she chose a Catholic School in Belgium. But Cecil was back in England before the war started, and rather surprisingly took a job as a trainee draper in Bobby's of Eastbourne, a superior department store. He said that he enjoyed learning about the different types of cloth. Maybe he had been speaking to his brother Charles. Cecil Schwabe, despite his considerable talents, was a shy and rather diffident soldier. He did not like Army life but did his best, and his great sense of humour carried him through, together with the joy of having his older brother Sydney for company.

As the war dragged on, things became very difficult for the Schwabes at home. The mood of the country was changing. With the increasing number of deaths and casualties suffered by British soldiers and civilians, the very name Schwabe, with its German-Jewish connotation brought unhappiness and suspicion. Despite the family's obvious loyalty to King and Country, bricks were thrown though the Albany's windows and worse, some who had been friends would ignore the family and pass them by without a word.

In December 1915, Charles August Schwabe died of stomach cancer, a sad end for a remarkable man who, at the time of his death had three of his eldest sons fighting in the British Army. For Kate, her husband's death could not have come at a worse time, but she took charge immediately, indeed she had already taken over the running of the Albany Hotel. She was determined to provide a proper home for her family and in particular for her young girls. Rosa, the youngest, was a feisty five year-old, a real handful. In addition to the girls, Kate's two younger sons Godfrey and Eric were still at school; they too would need a home. Kate was still only 45 and she would be breadwinner, father and mother to all her children. She was a remarkable person.

The Albany Hotel had to go. It was sold and then in a matter of weeks, Kate had taken over the management of The Alexandra Hotel in St Leonards on Sea, close to Hastings. It was a good move, there was room enough for the family and it had a small piece of land. That done, Kate told her children that they were to change their name to Parker and that none of them were to talk about it. It was to be a secret. Such was the force of Kate's personality that the majority of her family kept the secret for the rest of their lives.

While Sydney and Cecil were still training in Sussex with Lowther's Lambs, Charles had been promoted to a Captain in June 1915, and joined the 20th Battalion of the Royal Fusiliers which was shipped to France and deployed on the Western Front on 21st November 1915. Charles was to learn the news of his father's death when he himself had been wounded in the shoulder on his first tour of Front Line duty. It was a relatively minor injury but shortly afterwards on 16TH January the following year Charles, then working as a chemical adviser, was gassed and so ill that he was taken off strength for some three months. Charles' arrival on the Western Front had coincided with the first significant action in the war involving phosgene gas.

On 3rd July 1916 *The Gazette* announced that Captain Schwabe had been transferred to the General List. After that – nothing. He simply disappeared. In November 1918, the war over, there was still no news. Where had he gone and what was he doing? He had not been posted dead or missing. Had he been locked up or

TOP TO BOTTOM: *C. Schwabe, survived: S.P. Schwabe, killed 7/9/1918:*
H. Diplock, killed 21/4/1916: S. Creasey, killed 3/6/1916:
T.J. Ball, survived: R.S. Welchman, died of wounds 13/9/1916:
R. Lower, killed 1/8/1917

Officers and NCO's of the 12th Royal Sussex.
Bexhill, East Sussex 7th May 1915

captured by the enemy? His disappearance was a mystery.

In the meanwhile, on 19th March 1916, the 11th 12th and 13th Royal Sussex Battalions sailed for France via Le Havre just as Charles' Fusiliers had done a few months earlier. Sydney Schwabe, a respected sergeant in the 11TH, would have taken care to see that his brother Cecil was looked after during the voyage. Just before the battalions left for France, Lt Edmund Blunden (who became a famous war poet) joined the 11TH Battalion as a Lieutenant, the most dangerous of jobs; it would be his responsibility to lead his men over the top.

Sydney had been upset by the way his family had been scorned in Hastings for being German, and grieved for his father. What could he do to help? He had little or nothing to give but on 5th March 1916 he made and signed his will. So far he had been fortunate, but with his Battalion due to move to France, close to the Somme within in the next ten days he knew he would be lucky to survive.

In the event of my death I give the whole of my property and effects to my beloved mother Kate Schwabe residing at the Alexandra Hotel Hasting,

Signed SYDNEY PHILIP SCHWABE
Sergeant, the 11th Royal Sussex

On arrival in France the Royal Sussex were based at Richebourg where they became part of the 116th Infantry Division in Kitchener's New Army. The three battalions were given a reasonable amount of time for training, the weather was good, and conditions were rather better than either Sydney or Cecil had expected. All went well until the 30th June, when the Royal Sussex Battalions joined together to fight the infamous battle of the Boar's Head at Richebourg, L'Avoue.

The battle opened with British guns bombarding the German trenches. Then the 12th and the 13th Sussex Battalions went over the top (many for the first time) and under heavy fire attacked the enemy trenches, bombing and bayoneting their way in. The 11th Battalion supplied carrying parties. For a while the Sussex men succeeded in taking the German Front Line trenches, holding them for some four hours and, briefly, taking the second line trench, beating off repeated counter attacks. But, in the afternoon the men who had fought so hard had to withdraw, due to a shortage of ammunition and mounting casualties. The engagement was a disaster. In five hours the Royal Sussex lost 17 officers and 349 men all killed, including twelve sets of brothers. A further thousand men were wounded or taken prisoner. In the *Royal Sussex Regimental History*, the Battle of Boar's Head is known as 'THE DAY SUSSEX DIED.'

The following day the Battle of the Somme began; twenty thousand men died on the first day. Given the scale of losses at the Somme, I guess it is almost inevitable that the Royal Sussex action at Richebourg would be regarded as a mere side show by some historians. But it was much more than that. The loss of good men was over 50% in that one short battle. If such losses continued, the war with Germany would be lost.

Fortunately the two brothers survived their first battle. There was even a small mention about them in the local Hastings paper which, after congratulating Charles Schwabe on his promotion to a chemical adviser in France, mentioned that his two brothers, who had been in action the previous week, had come through safely.

But there was to be no let up for the 11th Sussex. On the 3rd September 1916 the battalion, together with units from the Hampshire Regiment and The Black Watch, was chosen for another attack, this time on the German Lines towards Beaumont Hamel close to the valley of the River Ancre. The aim was to roll back the enemy front line and facilitate the destruction of an enemy stronghold. At first the attack was successful with both the Sussex and the Hampshire men reaching and taking their objective, the enemy front line. But the Hampshire men had suffered too many casualties, and the Black Watch in the Ancre valley were overwhelmed by machine gun fire and driven back almost to their start line.

By the evening the attack was declared unsuccessful. The 11th Battalion alone had suffered 300 casualties, including Sergeant Sydney Schwabe who was very badly wounded and sent home. Cecil was distraught. It had been another truly terrible day for The Royal Sussex Regiment in France, which for all practical purposes had been destroyed by the enemy and could no longer be regarded as a fighting unit. All this was despite the best endeavours of the 6th Battalion of the Cheshire Brigade of Infantry doing its very best to provide cover for the Sussex men following their forced retreat back to their own trenches.

Lieutenant Edmund Blunden survived both battles unscathed despite leading his men over the top and joked that the only reason for his survival was his very small stature – he was easy to miss. But war left its mark on Edmund and his subsequent life was an unhappy one. Here is a verse he wrote about the battles of 1916

1916 SEEN FROM 1921

Tired with dull grief, grown old before my day,
I sit in solitude and only hear,
Long silent laughters, murmurings of dismay
The lost intensities of hope and fear;

In those old marshes yet the rifles lie,
On the thin breastwork flutter the grey rags,
The very books I read are there-and I
Dead as the men I loved, wait while life drags

Close to where Cecil and Sidney had fought their last battle together, a young Guards Officer, one Lieutenant Harold Macmillan was waiting in the British Lines of Beaumont Hamel for orders as to when he and his men would join Haig's offensive As it happened Macmillan and his men did not have to wait long. Exactly ten days after the defeat at the River Ancre the 2nd Grenadier Guards were ordered to advance with Macmillan leading his men over the top. Within an hour Macmillan had been wounded twice and a little later lay bleeding in a crater for many hours. Macmillan survived and went on the become Prime Minister. Here's what he had to say about bravery:

"Bravery is not really vanity, but a kind of concealed pride because everyone is watching you. Then I was safe, but alone and absolutely terrified because there was no need to show off any more, no need to pretend ... there was nobody for whom you were responsible, not even the stretcher bearers. Then I was very frightened ...I do remember the sudden feeling – you went through a whole battle for two days...suddenly there was nobody there ... you could cry if you wanted to..."

After Sydney had been sent home, Cecil too was wounded in the shoulder and was taken off strength. When he had recovered there was the question of what he should do. For all practical purposes the 11th Battalion was little more than a cadre. It was then that the Tank Corp made Cecil Schwabe an offer: If he joined the Tanks, he would be made an officer and given the job of dispatch rider. His duties would be to help direct tanks when engaged with the enemy and carry messages. 'Ours is a mobile war,' said one of the officers. Cecil Schwabe was delighted; it sounded interesting. Yes, he would be pleased to join, the last thing he wanted was to return to the bloody trenches.

But there was a problem, Cecil had never driven a motorcycle,

Second Leutenant Harold Macmillan, Grenadier Guards, France 1915

Edmund Blunden

Cecil's last post

he would have to learn. His first lesson was a disaster. The Instructing Sergeant filed the following report:

REPORT OF ACCIDENT
TO LIEUTENANT CECIL SCHWABE. 20th May 1918

I was out in a side car with the above officer who was riding a motorcycle for the first time and I was teaching him how to drive when he failed to take a bend in the road, lost control of his machine which crashed through a hedge, overturned and threw him some distance leaving him with injuries from which he is now suffering.

The injuries were severe, Lieutenant Schwabe's neck had been dislocated and it was only through the excellent care and attention that he received from one of the advanced casualty stations that he survived. 'Leave that man with us,' said the doctor in charge, when a party arrived to move patients to a safer unit further behind the lines, 'a move now will kill him.'

Miraculously 2nd Lt Cecil Schwabe of the Tank Corp survived his injuries and the war. When after some months he was released from hospital, Kate nursed him back to health in the Alexandra Hotel, encouraging him to work on a small piece of land adjoining the hotel. Cecil enjoyed the work and soon became very proud of his chickens.

There was some further good news for Cecil: On 4th November 1918, Douglas Haig, Commander in Chief of the British Armies in France, approved the accident report and the War Office granted him a 35% Army pension which he received every month of his

life until he died on 21st May 1971. The money was still being credited to Lieutenant Cecil Schwabe when almost everybody knew him as Cecil Parker, the actor.

But before the war was ended there was to be more sadness for the Schwabe family when one of their favourite sons, Sydney Philip Schwabe, lost his life in the closing months of the war. On recovering from his severe wounding at Beaumont Hamel he had joined the Royal West Surrey Regiment where he had been commissioned as a 2nd Lieutenant, It seems appropriate to quote the Hastings newspaper's announcement of his death.

SECOND LIEUTENANT S.P. SCHWABE

The announcement of the death of Second Lieutenant Sydney Philip Schwabe, son of Mrs Parker, Alexandra Hotel, St Leonards, will be received with deep regret by a large number of residents.

This young officer, who was just 23 years old, was educated at

Mr Francis Heath's School, Tudor Hall, Hawkhurst, and joined the Army in September 1914 as a Private in the 11th Royal Sussex Regiment (Lowther's Lambs). He rose to the rank of Sergeant, was badly wounded at Beaumont Hamel, and upon recovery took a commission in the Royal West Surrey Regiment. He went over to France for the second time on July 21st 1918, and was killed exactly four years from the day he joined the Army.

In a letter from a comrade, he says of Lieutenant Schwabe: "As a friend he was splendid, as a man so very straight, as a sportsman it has been an honour to be associated with him in every branch of sport. He has proved himself as a fine soldier and he will be greatly missed."

Sincere sympathy will be extended to Mrs Parker and her family in their very sad loss.

Lieutenant Sydney Philip Schwabe's body was buried close to where he fell, and later exhumed and moved to the main war Cemetery at Nurlu. Here another poem by Edmund Blunden which serves to illustrate the futility and sadness of that awful war

ESCAPE

A Colonel:
There are four officers, this message says,
Lying all dead at Mesnil.
One shell pitched clean amongst 'em at the foot
Of Jacob's Ladder. They're all Sussex men.
I fear poor Flood and Warne were of that party.
And the Brigade wants them identified . . .

A Mind:
Now God befriend me,
The next word not send me
To view those ravished trunks
And hips and blackened hunks.

A Colonel:
No, not you, Bunny, you've just now come down.
I've something else for you.
Orderly!
(Sir!)
Find Mr. Wrestman.

CHAPTER 3

CAPTAIN CHARLES SCHWABE IN ST PETERSBERG

In June 1915 Charles was promoted to a Captain in the 20th Battalion of The Fusiliers. In November of that year his Battalion sailed for France. Nervous, but in good spirits, on 21 November the Fusiliers took up their positions on the Western Front. They would show the Germans a thing or two. But, they were horrified at what they found: dead bodies, stinking trenches and mud everywhere. There would be little honour or glory for any of them that winter.

Captain Schwabe had a troubled start and for him things would get worse. Within a week of being on the Front Line he was struck in his shoulder by shrapnel; a minor injury, but painful. Then early in the New Year, working as a Chemical Adviser, he was gassed so badly that he was taken off strength for some three months. Charles' arrival on The Western Front had coincided with the first significant action in the war involving phosgene gas. Inhalation of phosgene could cause damage to victims' lungs and was agonising. Fortunately for Charles, he was strong and fit and there were no long-term problems.

Kate and the family heard little from Charles once he was in France other than the news that he had been promoted to a Chemical Advisor, a promotion which was confirmed in the local newspapers. Then on the 3rd July, the *Gazette* announced that

Captain Schwabe had been transferred to *The General List*. After that nothing more was heard either from him or the Army for the next two and a half years. Where had he gone and what was he doing? He had not been posted dead or missing. Had he been locked up or captured? His disappearance was a mystery.

Had any of Charles' family and friends been told that they might find him in Russia they would have been astonished and even more so to learn that in the summer of 1916 he had joined MI6 as a Secret Service Intelligence Officer.

MI6 (or MI1c as it was called during the 14 – 18 War) had been created and was managed by Mansfield Cumming, a Naval Officer who had retired early because of sea-sickness. Cumming was fond of carrying his sword stick with him; he wore a monocle and cut a singular figure in his black uniform with his broad shoulders. Charles had not been interviewed by Cumming but had been suddenly conscious of a big man staring at him when he was waiting to be seen by others in a crowded Whitehall Court, MI6's centre of operations.

All this took place at a very difficult time in the War. Russia was in a desperate state with over two million dead. If Russia were defeated, Germany would be able to transfer some 70 Divisions back to the Western Front. Everything had to be done, by fair means or foul, to keep Russia in the War. How could the use of gas help in this endeavour, a question Charles was asked for the umpteenth time by two officers who were interviewing him. 'Well, in the right conditions, it could help to slow an enemy advance but gas is tricky stuff to handle,' replied Captain Charles Schwabe. 'Well you had better see what you can do,' said the senior of the two officers. 'You appear to know more about the problem than anyone else we have seen.' Seven days later Captain Schwabe arrived in Russia. There had been no time to visit his family in Sussex first.

Captain Schwabe's base in St Petersburg was in offices close to the British Embassy, where to all appearances he was just another member of staff. One of his first assignments was to write a report for Lieutenant General Ipatieff Head of the Chemical Committee

St. Petersburg

of the Russian Imperial Army on gas warfare and investigate how prepared the Russian Army was to make, and defend itself, against such an attack. Charles may have suggested improvements to gas masks as the Russian models were very inefficient.

Charles could scarcely have imagined that things in Russia would be so bad: fighting and discontent everywhere with many close to starvation. Filthy streets with marvellous palaces left to rot and the war against Germany a bitter disaster. Everything was an unbelievable mess and as winter approached, the long queues of women searching for food grew longer. Charles, must have wondered what hope there was for this once great Nation, but he would do his best. Maybe gas could stop the Germans, but Charles didn't really believe it would.

In 1916 there was a Christmas party at the Embassy. With heating non-existent, Charles could never remember being so cold. There was little cheer except for some decent Scotch, and the party broke up early. The river Neva was frozen over and most of the street lights broken. He might just as well go back to work, he thought to himself, but then a friend told him that he had a spare ticket for the Marinsky Theatre to see the Ballet. The Tsar no longer visited, but the Royal Box sparkled in candlelight and Charles would have caught a glimpse of Imperial Russia as it once was.

When Charles arrived in Leningrad there was much talk about the Tsarina's relationship with her Holy Adviser Rasputin who had bought some relief to her son who was suffering from haemophilia. Rasputin was a very large frightening man who had many enemies. He had been criticised in the press for his behaviour: his orgies, his hold over the Royal family and for being pro-German. Many thought that if the Tsar and the Royal family were to survive then Rasputin would have to be eliminated. Charles had heard about Rasputin when he was with MI6 in London, and had to his astonishment, been told that MI6 might be prepared to lend assistance should an attempt be made on Rasputin's life.

Prince Felix Yusupov, an elite member of the Tsar's group of Pages, resolved that Rasputin must be dealt with and quickly, so with two close colleagues he undertook to assassinate 'the Monster.' The deed was done shortly before midnight on 29th December 1916 in Yusupov's Palace. It was a badly bungled murder; it took four bullets and two cakes of cyanide to finally dispatch Rasputin. The conspirators then dumped the mutilated body in a small patch of the Neva River which had not frozen over. The fourth and last bullet had been fired from an English revolver leading to a strong rumour that an English spy had been involved. Indeed years later it was revealed that the final fatal shot had been fired by one Lieutenant Oswald Rayner, a British Intelligence Officer from his ·45 Webley revolver. Rasputin and the Tzarina, who was of German origin, had lobbied to seek a peace treaty with Germany. British, French and USA policy at that time had been to keep the Russians in the war.

The murder made headline news across the world but did nothing to save the Royal family and in March Tsar Nicholas II announced his abdication. At first it seemed that was good news for the Allies. Prince Lvov was voted Prime Minister and Kerensky, a powerful politician, was made Minister of Justice. Kerensky was determined that the war against Germany be continued.

The new government moved quickly and a new eight point plan was agreed including an immediate amnesty for political prisoners. Kerensky was as good as his word and ordered that a new offensive be mounted against the German invaders. In the meanwhile Captain Schwabe continued his work advising the military on how gas might be used to defend Russia and perhaps attack the enemy. But he had little hope that anything would change while for all practical purposes the discredited Russian Officer class was still in charge.

But there were compensations for the young Captain. Charles, like his father August, much enjoyed company and despite the dangers of living in the city there were lots of parties where as well as male company there would be some pretty women, those who had lost their husbands in the war or were marooned in St Petersburg.

Among Charles' friends was the author Arthur Ransome, a left-wing socialist but one who had no time for the Bolsheviks. It was said that Ransome chose to live in Leningrad so he could live as far away as possible from his wife. On a personal note, I remember the pleasure I had from reading Arthur Ransome's *Swallows and Amazons* stories, *The Secret Water*, and others that my father bought me. Had he done that on the recommendation of his brother Charles? It would be nice to think so.

As the year of 1917 wore on the troubles in Russia intensified and as a result of the Amnesty for political prisoners Lenin was back in Leningrad. While the Bolsheviks were still one of the smaller political groups they knew exactly what they wanted: Peace with Germany, a world revolution, and an end to the British Empire in India.

In May it seemed that Kerensky might win the day and at a meeting of the Provisional Government Lenin was voted down and Kerensky was put in charge of the War Office and the Russian

Arthur Ransome in Russia

Navy. Captain Schwabe was still a junior member of the British team, but he was trusted by his superiors and knew that when Somerset Maugham, the author, arrived in St Petersburg that he was carrying funds for the Provisional Government. Charles got on well with Maugham and they became late night drinking companions. Charles thought that Tahiti sounded more fun than Russia!

Kerensky's Russian offensive against the Germans started with some success but collapsed when the Germans counter attacked and the battle became yet another catastrophic defeat for the Russian Army. Then as the year progressed the Bolsheviks' strength continued to grow. Lenin and his followers would stop at nothing to achieve their aims.

CHAPTER 4
LENIN TAKES OVER:
CHARLES SWIMS FOR HIS LIFE

On the 25th October there was another coup. The British Ambassador was looking out of his window when he saw that armoured cars had taken up positions all round the Winter Palace where Kerensky and his Ministers were holding a meeting. That evening the Peter and Paul Fortress fired a few shells into the Palace and by midnight the Bolsheviks were in control. Kerensky had to flee for his life, leaving Russia for America. Later Kerensky returned to Britain. He is buried at Putney Vale Cemetery in London, the resting place of a brave man.

But even after this latest upheaval no one party was in control of Russia; in many parts of that vast country things went on very much as they had done in the past. But in Russia's two great cities, Moscow and St Petersberg, now renamed Leningrad, the Bolsheviks were now the strongest party and in December, the Cheka, Lenin's hated but efficient secret police, were on the Streets of Petrograd.

By the end of 1917 Buchanan the British Ambassador had retired and returned to England. It had been an unhappy time for him but he had done his job and warned London many times of the dangers that Lenin and his Bolsheviks posed for the Western Powers. In the meanwhile, Captain Charles was still doing his best to try and help the Imperial Russian Army and submitting papers to General Schwartz, the officer in charge of the defence of Petrograd, on what might be done.

There was a good deal of surprise when Robert Bruce Lockhart was sent to Petrograd to replace Buchanan. Lockhart was a remarkable character. He was a Russian speaker, a womaniser, a sportsman and a brave and resourceful operator. Perhaps his charm was his greatest asset, even the Cheka seemed to like him. Astonishingly, Lockhart managed to persuade the Cheka to allow Moura Budberg, his lover, an aristocratic Russian, to leave Russia for England. The former Liberal Member of Parliament, Nick Clegg is related to her.

In the spring of 1918 there was little improvement in the supply of food and the standard of living for ordinary Russian people became even worse with some agricultural workers holding on to their produce. At the same time thousands of army deserters roamed the streets while the Cheka would break into homes and offices searching for those who opposed their revolution.

In May Charles was asked to contact the New Assistant Military Attaché for the United States Embassy, Peter Bukowski. Bukowski had been given funds to plan the 'evacuation of materials' which would have included the British Gas stocks. The two of them became friends. Bukowski reported that the Bolsheviks now considered Germany a much greater threat to their existence than the Allies because of the Brest-Litovsk's harsh terms and also because of the initial success of Germany's long-awaited spring offensive on the Western Front in France.

But that moment soon passed and before long the Bolsheviks again regarded the Western Allies as their real enemy. And so it was that the majority of the valuable supplies which had been collected together was for the most part left to rot.

With Kerensky gone there were endless discussions on what should be done and who the Allies should support. There were plots and counter plots but no easy answers. Perhaps the best thing to do would be to assassinate Lenin and send a large body of well trained troops with artillery to Archangel. Gas bombs were sent but only six tanks. The unpalatable truth was that if Russia was to be governed by Lenin, then like it or not Russia would be our enemy.

On 30th August 1918 the British and the French Embassies in Petrograd were sacked by a strong force of militant Bolsheviks supported by the Cheka. The British Naval Attaché, Captain Crombie, was shot and killed, his body left lying in the entrance of the Embassy in a pool of blood. Forty staff were arrested but then, after some twelve hours, much to their surprise, released. But the Cheka knew what they were doing and within a few hours the Allied plots against Russia and the Bolsheviks were on the front page of every newspaper. Once the news was released, the Embassy staff were again arrested but this time incarcerated in a decaying fortress on an island in the Neva River, The ancient Peter and Paul Fortress.

The attack on the two Embassies had come as some surprise. There had been no warning but there was a perception that the French and English had in some way been involved with an attempt on Lenin's life and also in the assassination of Moisie Uritsky, the Head of the Petrograd Cheka on 17th August 1918. It appears Arthur Ransome got wind of the purge as he fled the country some four days earlier, but he recorded the event and intimated that foreign nationals including embassy staff were rounded up as 'bargaining chips' in the event that Russian hostages were taken in any attempted coup. Ronald Cambers' comprehensive biography *The Double Life of Arthur Ransome* demonstrates that these were particularly tense and troubled times.

Charles was finally arrested with Bruce Lockhart and others from the MI6 Offices on the Moika Embankment. Life in the Fortress was terrifying. In three short weeks some five hundred political prisoners were executed. Waiting for death they were held in medieval type-dungeons. It seemed to the British prisoners that there would be no reprieve. But one Captain Schwabe was not going to give up. Somehow he got outside the Fortress and braving the fast flowing current of the river Neva

St Paul and St Peter Fortess, Petrograd

swam to the river bank and made good his escape. 'Sink or Swim' his father had said while teaching his young son to swim. Charles had learnt his lesson.

After some very anxious days for the British prisoners held in the Fortress, the British Government reached an agreement on an exchange of prisoners to take place at the end of September. The British prisoners to be exchanged included Captain Schwabe, but nobody seemed to know where he was.

Charles, despite the Neva's cold water and its fast flowing current, had managed to reach the river's bank and under cover of night found his way to the American Embassy. The Americans had been moved out due to the approach of the German Army, but Charles was lucky, a clerk, Karin Sante had been left in charge and Peter Bukowski instructed Karin to give Charles shelter, an order which almost certainly saved Charles' life. Then, a day or two later, again at night, Charles left the American Embassy and made his way to Finland, swimming the frontier stream between the two countries.

In Finland Charles would have been delighted to meet up with his colleagues all fit and well and lucky to escape with their lives. There was of course much unfinished business which Captain

Schwabe would have regretted, particularly the 50,000 shells of toxic gas that had been left in Archangel.

Safely back in Britain, Charles Parker Schwabe was released from Service on 4th February 1919 and went home to Bolton. He had done his best and his efforts were acknowledged in a notice posted from St James Palace on 22nd March 1919.

The King has been graciously pleased to give orders for the following appointment of the Most Excellent Order of the British Empire for valuable services rendered in connection with military operations in North Russia.

CHAPTER 5

THE GIRLS THE BOYS LEFT BEHIND

It is 1919, the War is over and Charles, back from Russia, has been de-mobbed, but it would have been a sad and bewildered Schwabe family back together at the Alexandra Hotel. Their much loved brother Sydney Philip had been killed and poor Cecil, with his dislocated neck, was struggling to keep the grounds of their new home in some kind of order. The Albany, where the family had spent their childhood, was now owned by someone else

It was all very unsettling. Moreover, in the middle of the War, on the instruction of their mother, the family had all been told to change their name from Schwabe to Parker. 'I don't see why,' complained Rosa the youngest of Kate's daughters. 'Because it's important,' said Kate. Rosa knew better than start an argument. 'The change is to remain a secret,' Kate continued, 'and if anybody asks you, tell them that the Government thought it was a good idea because Philip, Cecil and Charles have been so brave fighting for Britain.' The secret was well kept down the years.

I had a shock when I first saw a copy of August's Death Certificate. It seemed so final and awful for him to die of stomach cancer; what an indignity for the man.

He must have wondered as he lay dying whether his sons would survive. The War had begun badly for the Allies and August was conscious of a growing anti-German sentiment as the lists of British dead and wounded soldiers were published on a

Kay Parker with her father, Charles August Schwabe

The Schwabe sisters.
Standing at the back (LEFT TO RIGHT) *are Margery & Sally, in the front row*
(LEFT TO RIGHT) *are Audrey, Kathleen, Dorothea & Rosa.*

daily basis. Indeed, some of his acquaintances would no longer speak to him. 'Don't take any notice,' said his friend Conan Doyle. But unlike August, Conan was fit and well and, was not German. So what about Kate's girls? There were six of them, and although in different ways, their lives were just as badly affected by the War as those of their five brothers.

Kate's eldest daughter Dorothea married Ernest David Campbell and then emigrated to Argentina where Ernest owned a substantial Estancia in the heart of that vast country. Dorothea, known as Dot, was the one Aunt I never met, but evidently she was well liked and popular in the family. Cecil told me that he had once taken his wife Muriel to visit Dot and Ernest at their Estancia in Argentina. It was in the early 60s and it was not an easy undertaking: It was a two-day drive from Buenos Aires and the roads were appalling. Unhappily, Muriel was car-sick all the way there and all the way back. But they found Ernest's Estancia, astonishing for its size and order and it seemed that as far as their eyes could see it was all 'their land.'

In later years Beth and I had the pleasure of meeting Elaine, Dot's daughter, on one of her occasional visits to England. We liked her. Sadly things were not going too well for her family, the near bankruptcy of the country and its revolutions had taken their toll, money was short and it was difficult for her children to find jobs. Elaine died in 2008.

The only other daughter of Kate's to marry was Kathleen. Kathleen Schwabe was born in 1899. A strong-minded young lady, while working in the Hastings Council Offices she fell in love with one Francis Henry Carrington Pickering. He was not perhaps the kind of man one might expect to find in Hastings. Theirs was a passionate affair and they were soon married and had their first child, a son Richard. Richard grew up to be a fine young man who later became a pilot in The Royal Air Force. Kathleen, or Kay as she was called, and Frank had two further children, Michael born in 1926 and Daphne in 1928.

Uncle Frank was a charming man and good fun. With such a

A Lysander Aircraft

Francis Pickering

name it was unsurprising to learn that his family had money, but Frank's misfortune was that he was not too good at making it on his own account. It seems he was something of an adventurer. His first job was as a tea planter in India before returning to England and joining the British Army where he was made a Lieutenant. Daphne tells me, her father, in common the Schwabe men, was

Kathleen Pickering

Richard Pickering

reticent and rarely confided in anyone, least of all his family.

In the 1920's Frank joined the Hudson Bay Company and became a furrier. It was not the best choice of career at the time but he was indeed unlucky that his London shop was destroyed by enemy bombing in the 1940's. Frank, seemingly unconcerned, rejoined the Services, this time the Royal Air Force. He was sent to North Wales where he remained for most of the war helping look after squadrons of Lysander Aircraft. I suspect that Frank rather enjoyed himself living in the Officers' Mess in North Wales, but things were not so easy for Kay and the children. Their house in Mill Hill was requisitioned as an Officers Mess. There was no alternative for Kay and the two younger children, but to spend much of their time at Copse Hanger with Margery, Sally and Godfrey. Still, holidays in North Wales during the war were quite a bonus

As my parents' house in Radlett was not far from Mill Hill, I saw quite a bit of Kathleen, who I always addressed as Auntie Kay, after the war. She was always very hospitable, a great cook who would provide the most splendid spreads for her parties, so I was surprised when Daphne told me that when she was first married she was bullied by her mother-in-law Marion Pickering for being useless in the kitchen. 'Well, if you live in a hotel, as Kay did for many years, you are not expected to do the cooking'.

Kay was always kind and helpful. I remember calling in at her house in the early 1950's on my way home. I was very short of money, petrol and food but Auntie Kay made me welcome. She gave me £5 for some petrol (a lot of money in those days), a slap-up tea and a large bag of little cakes and sandwiches. Now, sixty years on, I am not sure that I even thanked her.

A party at Kay and Frank's really was something and the two I attended were memorable. The food and how it was displayed, the drinks, everything one could wish for. But it was Frank I best remember, for his party spirit, his acting as a priest wearing a bowler which he had adapted into a clerical hat. He told me I should read Kipling's poems and then recited two of them, word perfect with the right accent:

> *Though I have belted you and flayed you*
> *By The Livin Gawd that made you.*
> *You're a better man than I am Gunga Din*

50

And goodness knows why I remember but Frank told me of the poem Kipling wrote about his son Jack. I had to look this one up, but here's a verse

Have you any news of my boy Jack?
Not this tide
When do you think he'll come back?
Not with this wind blowing and the tide

I don't think I saw Frank again after that party until my father took me to see him in hospital when he was very ill. Things had been difficult for Frank after the war but Dad had managed to find him a job in the Mill Hill offices of ICI. Frank's walking stick lay on the floor near his hospital bed. 'Give it to me Eric,' he said and smiled, 'when I want help I bang on the floor.' As well as being a humorous man, he was a brave one.

I can only remember seeing Richard, 'Dick', Kay's eldest son, on one occasion when he came to our house in Radlett. He was looking very smart in his pilot officer's uniform. Dick was my brother James' God-father and it was desperately sad news to learn that he had been killed flying his RAF Mosquito over occupied France. It is believed he was helping the partisans.

Michael Pickering, Kay's second son, was a very gentle person and a scholar. He joined the Navy in the later part of the war and was on board an aircraft carrier sailing for the Far East when the two atomic bombs were dropped on Japan and the war came to an end. Michael and I sometimes met up in London. We got on well. Later Michael married Joan Hall and inherited four step-sons: Ralph, Robert, Denise and Bernard.

The youngest of Frank and Kay's three children was of course Daphne.

After Frank died Kay moved house to be near Rosa with the idea that they might be able to help one another. Sadly it didn't work out as Kay suffered a stroke. Daphne returned from Africa to nurse her. Then Rosa got cancer and was nursed by Audrey.

Daphne Marion Carrington Pickerington, for that was the full

Daphne Kavanagh

Michael Pickering

name her parents gave her, is still alive and well. Daphne married a Richard John Kavanagh, a delightful man and keen Rugby player and for some years the two of them lived and worked in Tanzania. They had two children Katherine and Alison. Sadly Richard died in 2006.

Then there were our four maiden aunts – Margery, Sally, Audrey and Rosa. Sadly they were part of a legion of young women whose fiancés or prospective husbands were lost on the

Kate Parker

battlefields, at sea or in the air during the First World War. Grandma Kate continued to provide a home for all of them until 1939, but it would be quite wrong to suggest that they were four ladies of leisure be-moaning their fate or waiting for something to turn up; nothing could be further from the truth.

The eldest of the four sisters was Marjorie and it is perhaps her life which started with the most promise. When I first knew her she was running a kindergarten school in Godalming, Surrey, where she lived in a small house with Sally and Audrey. Initially I found her formidable, she seemed impatient and our conversation was confined to question and answers. But I soon found that Margery, like most of the Parker family, had a great sense of humour – one of our family's strengths – and we got on well.

Margery had started out in life with the ambition of becoming a concert pianist and indeed she had her own concert at the Wigmore Hall in London. She was doing well before severe arthritis put an end to her career. Sadly she lived in much pain for the rest of her life but continued to do her best and became an excellent teacher running her own nursery school. Once Margery

The end of the Albany Hotel.
A number of Hussars were killed in the bombing of the Albany Hotel and the Queens Hotel. The mess hall was located in the Albany Hotel.
The Albany Hotel was hit by a bomb dropped by a Focke Wolf 190 on 23ʳᵈ May 1943. This early afternoon raid, carried out by 10 aircraft was the second worst of the war in Hastings, resulting in the deaths of 25 and injuring 85 others.

A plaque on the site reads:
Eleven members of the 17ᵗʰ Duke of York's Royal Canadian Huzzars were killed in the bombing raid on the Albany Hotel 23ʳᵈ May 1943

told me rather wistfully, 'You know Tim, the war was difficult for us girls; it took away too many of our boys.' I was moved that she should confide in me.

Margery's younger sister Elsie, but known by everyone, family and friends, as Sally, lived with her for many years. Although Sally's face was very lined and drawn by the time I met her, it was clear that when young she would have been a vivacious and attractive young woman. When the war started she was engaged to be married to a member of the Searcy family, a famous name in catering, but her young man, like many others, died on the Western Front. When I knew Sally she had a job as a book-keeper for a firm in Godalming and caught the bus to and from work until she was in her seventies. I never really knew Sally, but she had a splendid laugh and gave my daughter Donna a wonderful sketch of a horse which she had drawn. Instinctively I liked Sally. I wish I had known her better.

The third sister living with Margery and Sally was Audrey. My father, Eric Parker, told me that just after the war Audrey had turned down her fiancé when he had proposed an early marriage. On being told it was all over the unfortunate young man declared that he would jump off Westminster Bridge. 'Did he jump?' I asked. 'Of course not,' my father replied, 'he was a right chump and Audrey is better off without him.' For a number of years Audrey was a Matron at the well-known Aysgarth School in Yorkshire. Later she moved to Charterhouse where she was known as the Green Dragon.

The youngest of Kate and August's children was Rosa. Rosa did not live in Godalming but struck out on her own as a vet and established a thriving practice in Mill Hill where Auntie Kay lived with Uncle Frank. Kay gave Rosa a great deal of help and encouragement in all kinds of ways. All was going well, Rosa was employing four qualified veterinary nurses until new government legislation decreed that as Rosa was not properly qualified, her practice was be shut down. What a bombshell. There were many tears but her friends, customers and supporters organised petitions to let her continue her practice and quite remarkably they won the day.

Sadly Rosa died young from lung cancer. She was in every sense a character, it was said that she much preferred her animals to people, she was a chain smoker with an odd sense of humour and she certainly stood up to my mother, another Kathleen, who tended to be bossy. How can I forget the great occasion when my mother gave a Christmas party? Rosa had been drinking, not too much, but enough, and distinguished herself by falling fast asleep with her head in a soup plate. 'My God!' my mother exclaimed, 'Eric – do something!'

CHAPTER 6

CAPTAIN CHARLES
BACK ON CIVVY STREET

So far we have looked at Charles' war record, but what happened in civilian life after the war had ended? After the First World War, Charles returned to Bolton working for James Hardcastle, a cotton finishing company specialising in printed fabrics where he became managing director. He was not only a talented chemist but also spoke Russian and German fluently and was an exceptional pianist who could play any tune by ear. He was very sociable and on his business trips to America he was renowned for entertaining the passengers after dinner on the Queen Mary. In 1921 he married Phyllis Coates of the Coates cotton family and they had two children, Dennis and Neil. It was a tragedy that Phyllis at a young age following a routine medical examination leaving the two young boys for a time without a mother. An unsettling time for both of them

During the Second World War the James Hardcastle company was engaged in printing maps to be hidden on the inside of garment linings to be used by intelligence personnel operating covertly behind enemy lines. Back in Bolton Charles took an active interest in all that was going on and contributed to the local Territorial Army. But, there were still tensions and there was a suspicion that Charles was a German sympathiser. Nothing could be further than the truth and the rumour was publicly rebuffed in

Dennis Parker

the Bolton Times.

Of the two children from Charles' first marriage, Dennis b1922 was perhaps the most highly decorated family member serving in the Second World War as an RAF fighter pilot. He was awarded the DFC (Distinguished Flying Cross) for acts of valour, courage and devotion to duty as a Flight Lieutenant. The official record showed he had '5 kills'. What the official report did not say is that part of Dennis' service was spent on the North Sea Convoys, the most hazardous of postings. He was 'demobbed' as Squadron Leader. Dennis was also an exceptional sportsman playing rugby for London Blackheath and selected for trials for England. Dennis was also an accomplished horseman who used to exercise race horses on the Downs for many years while working in London. Following in his father's industry, Dennis went on to become Chief Executive of Whitecroft Holdings a collection of cotton printing companies who huddled together for mutual support during the declining years of the industry, a thankless task for even the most valiant leader which was to precipitate a nervous breakdown from which he never fully recovered.

Dennis married Elizabeth Race in 1950 and they had two children Richard and Suzanne. Richard (Ricci) runs a successful removal company in Harpenden and Suzanne a very talented youth golfer, the English Girl's Golf Youth Championships, developed schizophrenia and is cared for in assisted accommodation. Ricci married Pamela Jackson and has a daughter Claire.

The other son Neil b1926 joined the Fleet Air Arm in the war and after became an investigative journalist for leading national papers and Reuters. He was a sensitive individual whom we met just a few times, and I attended his wedding. Sadly the marriage did not last. Whether trauma or some underlying condition, he took his own life shortly afterwards.

Charles subsequently married Leonie Horton in 1936. They had three children, Vanessa the eldest studied history at Cambridge and went on to gain a PhD. As an economic and architectural historian. Her book on *The Makings of Kings Lynn* is still held as a seminal work. She married Brian Doe in 1973 who

Charles Schwabe married Leonie Horton at Cartmel Priory in 1936

was both an Army architect and an archeologist specialising in the Middle East. Julian went to sea and became a master mariner before coming ashore to run the newly formed Nautical Institute. He married Christine de Mestral and they have two children Nicholas and Sonja. Quentin the youngest of the three children had a successful career as a weapons engineer officer in the Royal Navy and a further period as a project engineer in naval construction. He married Elizabeth Howard in 1982 and they had two children Jonathan and Charles. Sadly Charles' marriage to Leonie did not last and they were divorced, with unsettling consequences.

Charles was clearly a pre-eminent chemist and during his time with James Hardcastle and Co in Bolton he produced a string of cotton finishing patents and many original print processes which were used to supply gorgeous richly coloured prints to such outlets as Liberty's of London and Tootal fabrics. Towards the end of his life he was appointed chairman of the Bleachers Association, a position which reflected the esteem in which he was held within the cotton finishing business. Charles died in 1957.

CHAPTER 7

CECIL SCHWABE PARKER

In November 1918 the World War in Europe was over. Somehow Cecil, much to his own surprise and that of his family, was still alive, His dislocated neck was still giving him trouble but it was, he thought, a little better. It had been a good idea of his mother's to encourage her injured son to work the small patch of ground adjoining the Alexandra hotel. Cecil enjoyed himself – the work was within his compass – and on warm sunny days he was beginning to forget his aches and pains. He had become proud of his chickens, "my eggs are top quality," he told his friends and customers.

His mother Kate had wanted him to change his name to Parker with the rest of the family and to drop the name of Schwabe. "No I will keep the name," he told his mother, "I want to make quite sure the Army pays my dues." His mother could hardly quarrel with his logic but perhaps, like his brother Godfrey, Cecil had been proud of his father and wanted to keep things as they were. And why should he change his name when his friend and brother Philip Schwabe, who had been killed just weeks before the bloody war had ended, had never been given the chance to change his?

In 1919 Cecil was just over 21 years of age, by then he had spent four years at School in Belgium and four years in the Army. Feeling better and thinking there was something more to life than chickens and growing greens, he joined an amateur dramatic group in Hastings as a song and dance man. He much enjoyed

Cecil Schwabe

himself and that modest start proved to be the beginning of a glittering career with Cecil making his professional debut at the Eastbourne Devonshire Park Theatre in 1922. Three years later he made his first appearance in a West End production, as a member of the Liverpool Repertory Company. Muriel Ann Randall Brown was his leading lady. Cecil and Muriel were married in 1927 and

Cecil and Muriel Parker boarding a plane for Hollywood

their daughter Angela was born in 1928.

Cecil's career is well documented and there is no room in this story of the Schwabe-Parker family to list his many achievements. Suffice to say, he was never short of work until the day he died. Cecil's last film, which was shot in Brighton was 'Oh What A Lovely War' and after his retirement he moved the family to Brighton, a town he loved. A homecoming after an extraordinary career. What follows are my memories of a gentle, courteous man, a little shy, but with a great sense of humour. He was fun to be with and everybody who knew him, liked him.

Cecil was my father's brother and my Godfather. He and Muriel were always very kind to me and for some years towards the end of the Second World War our two families lived close to one another in Radlett, a village to the north of London. It had, and maybe still has, just one cinema – Radlett's House of Comfort. That makes me smile or perhaps it's the memory of a heavy-weight dance teacher who hired a hall adjoining the cinema. "Hold me tighter Tim!" That required courage!

When Cecil was not working he often came round in the evening for a game of darts. I was about 14 at the time. There would be fierce competition between my father, Cecil and me. I'll never forget one particular evening when, to Cecil's delight (he usually lost), he finished the game in great style: 19, triple 20 and double top. There were more than the usual number of whiskeys drunk that evening. Thinking about drink, I cannot think of any member of the Schwabe family who did not like his or her tot.

Cecil had a puckish sense of humour. In the 1940's food rationing was severe and the country, despite the war being over, was still being urged to 'Dig for Victory.' Many who had the space kept chickens and Cecil prided himself on his flock. In addition he grew rhubarb, new potatoes, broad beans and enormous quantities of green beans. One day James and I were invited round to see some of his new birds which had just been delivered. "They are really beautiful birds," he said and they were indeed very colourful. "I give my chickens the best of everything," he told us, "and lots of grit to make sure the eggs don't break. Here I will show you." He held one of his eggs in the air and dropped it in the grass where it broke. He dropped another and that too broke. He laughed and gave us two eggs to take home to our mother together with four large sticks of green/red rhubarb. "You better tell your mother that the eggs will be difficult to break. Oh and tell her to put plenty of sugar with the rhubarb."

Cecil and my father were always very good friends and sometimes our two families would meet on holiday. One year we were all staying in St Maw's in Cornwall and Cecil, by then quite a celebrity, was asked to crown the Carnival Queen, a very pretty girl with a grand coiffure of blond hair. The competition over, the band played and the new Queen sat on her throne. Cecil with a broad smile and just a little too merry, plonked a very spiky crown upside down on the Queen's head. The spikes became entangled with her hair. Cecil pulled the crown one way, the Mayor stepped forward and pulled in another direction and it was not until the Queen's mother clambered on to the stage and lent a hand that the crown, amid cheers, was pulled free and set to rights. The band played yet another Floral Dance and the Beauty Queen who had smiled throughout her ordeal, kissed Cecil firmly on the lips. "The lucky dog," muttered my father with a sideways glance at my mother.

Cecil never told me about the First World War and despite learning a bit about it at school I never asked. Perhaps I sensed it was not a subject that he would want to talk about. But he did tell me about the time during the Second World War when he was starring in Noel Coward's *Blithe Spirit* in the West End. London was still, from time to time, being bombed by the Germans. "When there was an air raid warning," Cecil said, "we would interrupt the play so that those who wanted to could take shelter. A surprising number of theatre goers would ignore the warning and so the cast would go on stage to entertain them. I would play the piano and the audience would join in; we had some marvellous times. Then when the all clear sounded we would carry on and finish the play".

There is perhaps one of Cecil's films I should mention, the 1945 film *Caesar and Cleopatra* staring Claude Rains as Caesar, Vivien Lee as Cleopatra and Douglas Fairbanks as Antony. My mother borrowed my father's green Standard and drove to London to take James and I to see "Uncle Cecil's latest smash hit film." Mum parked in Selfridges car park (for no charge) and we walked to the Cumberland Hotel where we had a 5-shilling lunch, the maximum restaurants were allowed to charge. Then it was off to the Odeon Marble Arch to see our uncle on the big screen. The film was never a smash hit and we had to wait a long time for Cecil to appear in the small supporting role of Britannus. But, his getting some of the best lines in such a prestigious film helped secure his position as an international star. After the film we went to the Lyons Corner House for tea or was it an ice cream? I can't remember.

When writing about Cecil it is only right to include Muriel, his wife, a very accomplished actress who gave up her career to support Cecil's. Muriel was the daughter of a successful Scottish glove maker and was a lady of the most remarkable charm. One day she asked me to drive her to Gatwick as she wanted to pay a last visit to an old friend in Edinburgh. I carried her luggage to the departure lounge but could go no further. There were no porters to be seen. "Don't you worry, Tim, just watch." Very soon a four ringed captain passed by, she tapped him on the shoulder and smiled. Without a moment's hesitation, the Captain picked up her bags and the two of them sailed through Customs.

In the last two years of his life Cecil was in and out of hospital with bronchitis and a heart problem. On one occasion he was hospitalised in one of the general wards of the Royal Sussex Hospital. I took Muriel to see him. "We must get him out of here and into a private hospital, he pays more than enough insurance," she told me. But Cecil would have none of it. In the next bed there was an ex-soldier called Charlie. The two of them had been in the trenches together on the Somme and were happily exchanging cigarettes. Muriel decided to leave Cecil where he was. 'I want him to be happy,' she said.

Cecil died on 21st September 1972, a remarkable and much-loved man. And he had some nice ideas. He once told me that it

Ingrid Bergman and Cecil Parker in the 1958 film 'Indiscreet'

was in everyones duty to spend their money. "That's what makes the world go round," he said, and that from a man who had for some years had paid tax at the rate of 95 pence in the pound.

Here is a short poem I found with Cecil's papers written for his wife Muriel.

> *Just to remind you if ever I find you*
> *Starting to linger and point a gloved finger*
> *At something expensive in France*
> *There are no English banks*
> *And I haven't the francs*
> *So my darling you haven't a chance*
> *But if in a boutique*
> *You see something unique*
> *That you know is a must*
> *Just lend me the money*
> *And then my dear Honey*
> *Let the bloody economy bust*

CHAPTER 8

GODFREY ARTHUR SCHWABE

Godfrey was known as Gas by his many friends, but how many of them knew that when he started out in life his surname had been Schwabe and his father a German? Godfrey grew up to be a likable, popular man, very clever with an inquiring mind, and a great sense of humour. He was a man of many parts: A father, a business man, a musician, an engineer and a sportsman. He was very tall, about 6ft 5" and had the most extraordinarily long fingers. Like most of the Parkers he was mainly bald but he stood out with his kindly face, his laugh and his infectious enthusiasm.

He was born in June 1901 in Hastings, the eighth child of Kate and Charles Schwabe. He would have had a happy childhood and there would have been little hint that thirteen years after his birth there would be a terrible war with his father's newly adopted country fighting against Germany.

Godfrey was at school in Hawkhurst, a minor public school, when the First World War started but as soon as he turned sixteen he left home and made for Liverpool where he became an engineering apprentice with the Camel Laird Ship Company in Birkenhead. Unfortunately there were workers in the shipyard who, knowing he was a German, bullied Godfrey Schwabe and on one occasion he was badly beaten up. While he had a miserable time there is no doubt that he would have stood up to his bullies. At the end of his apprenticeship he passed his exams

71

with distinction.

It is an interesting side to Godfrey's character that when the war was over and his mother Kate had changed the family name from Schwabe to Parker he kept his name and for many years called himself Schwabe-Parker. Did he want to show those who had bullied him that he didn't care, or perhaps he wanted to acknowledge his pride in his father for the bravery he had shown when everything was going against him? But, whatever the reason, there was a stubborn streak in the man together with his good humour and love of his family.

Godfrey Schwabe-Parker would have been pleased to say goodbye to Liverpool but while there he had become fascinated with the technology of cable laying ships connecting the old world with the new. So that he could learn more, when he finished at Camel Laird, he joined the Merchant Navy and went to sea as an engineering officer in one of the large cable laying vessels. We don't have a record of the name of his ship but Sara has a picture of Godfrey playing the banjo in the Ship's Band where he was known as King Banjo of Gazootland. Quite where Gazootland is and if there has ever been such a place I have still to find out.

By all accounts Godfrey much enjoyed his time at sea but his next job was to be very different. He accepted an opportunity to live in the Sudan and work on the irrigation of its extensive cotton fields. Godfrey soon grew to love the Sudan and its people and there was the added bonus that he had plenty of time to play polo and ride horses. Godfrey soon become an expert horseman and made many good friends including the Wall family who were to become godparents to his children Sara and Judy. On his periodic home leave Godfrey kept in touch with his family and went so far as to buy Copse Hanger a nice house close to The Red House where his mother and some of his sisters had moved after leaving Hastings. Later Kate moved into Copse Hanger and it was there my one and only meeting with my grandmother took place.

I guess it must have been in the late 1930's. She was sitting in a

The sanatorium at Davos, Switzerland where Godfrey was cured on TB, a cure recommended by Arthur Conan Doyle.

chair dressed all in black. I was most impressed by her large ear trumpet. I was invited to speak to her through her trumpet. I can't recall what I said, nor do I remember that she even responded, not a word, nor a smile. Within a minute or two I was ushered out of the room; my interview was over.

Before returning to Britain, Godfrey had a scare when he contacted TB. In those days the cure was to go to Davos in Switzerland for the air and its climate. It didn't always work, but Godfrey was cured. If Conan Doyle had still been alive, Godfrey would have thanked his father's old friend with all his heart.

In 1939 with another war against Germany in prospect Godfrey returned to live in Britain and met Gwendoline, a very pretty farmer's daughter living close to Godalming who he asked to be his bride. Engaged to be married, Godfrey needed his house back, but by then his mother, Kate, had little or no money left and her daughters no more than they could earn. It was a difficult time, but Godfrey with typical generosity guaranteed a home would be found for them and together with help from his three brothers Eric, Cecil and Charles Parker the deed was done. Godfrey took care of his sisters all his life. As often as possible on

73

Godfrey and Gwendolyn

Saturday mornings he would take Sara and Judy and the Aunts, as the children called them, to the Strathmore Café in Godalming. They would all have tea and cakes and as often as not, Sara and Judy would see their father pass one of the sisters a brown envelope, it was money to pay the rent and keep them going.

Godfrey Arthur Schwabe

Godfrey married Gwendoline in 1946 and Sara Kate was born later that year 1946, followed by Judy Kate in 1948, two Jewish names. Was that just a coincidence? I guess we will never know the answer. It is sad that both Sara and Judy had little time to know their father who died when he was just sixty five in 1966. It seems that he was always very busy, often working the better part of a six day week. But, that said he became a remarkably successful business man in the 1950's and 1960's. He was appointed a Director of M.C. Layton, a large machine tool merchant and for a

Godfrey Arthur Schwabe

time was Chairman of the Machine Tool Merchants Association. He and Gwen were good hosts and Godfrey returning home after Association Dinners, would tell Sara and Judy the latest Christine Keeler and Mandy Rice Davis jokes.

Godfrey was a man of great energy always dashing from one place to another but Sara and Judy tell me that he had a gentle and patient side, doing his best to help others and in particular Neil Parker, a cousin, one of Charles Parker's sons. Neil would arrive on his motor cycle with little or no warning and Godfrey would listen to him for hours. Neil was a journalist, a schoolmaster and a first class Rugby player but sadly he was a depressive who found life very difficult. Dennis Parker was another regular visitor. On his arrival Dennis and Godfrey would go out riding and in the evening play the piano together. Sara remembers Copse Hanger would become alive with music and laughter – 'they were great evenings' she told me.

In the 1950's I got to know my Uncle Godfrey pretty well – or thought I did – as for the better part of two years we would often catch the same bus from Waterloo station to Victoria. We became good friends and were of one accord when it came to buses. The best seats to be had were right up front on the top deck. It was an interesting ride, we crossed the River Thames over Lambeth Bridge and saw the barges and river traffic. One day, as our bus travelled round the back of the Army & Navy Stores, a topless girl glared at us from her bedroom window. Surreptitiously, we would look out for her on our subsequent bus rides but we never saw her again. The journey would take some 20 minutes before we disembarked – a word from his seafaring days Godfrey liked to use – at Victoria. We then walked to our respective offices, Godfrey to Grosvenor Gardens and me to Buckingham Palace Road where I was employed as a very junior buyer by Imperial Chemical Industries (ICI).

On our journeys together we talked of many things: About his work as an engineer, his life in the merchant navy and of the Sudan which he had loved. He told me about Gwen and Sara and Judy of whom he was very proud, about his riding and playing polo. But it was not a one sided conversation, he took a keen interest in what James and I had been doing and was my father still playing cricket? From time to time Godfrey would invite me to lunch at his favourite Polish restaurant in Grosvenor Square. Looking back I think he was concerned about what he considered my woeful education. He tried to help: a slide rule for Christmas, some tools that might be useful and even written instructions on how my elderly Morris should be de-coked. I still have the slide rule; it has never been used, but I keep it safe.

I still see him in my mind's eye and remember when I saw him after the war in uniform as a special constable at the Pepper Harrow Point to Point. He and a number of other police were being inspected by their Chief Constable. Godfrey stood in the front rank, head and shoulders the tallest man on parade.

'What on earth are you doing here Parker?' the Chief constable asked.

'I am here on duty, Sir'

'Well stand up straight.'

And with that both men burst into fits of hopeless laughter.

The last time I saw Godfrey was on the occasion when General De Gaulle placed a wreath on the French Memorial in Grosvenor Square. Other than General De Gaulle, the only other head one could see was Godfrey's. God bless him.

CHAPTER 9
ERIC JAMES CROFT PARKER

Eric was the youngest of the Schwabe brothers. He was born in 1903, and was father to James and myself. He was a kind and generous man and like many of the family a good sportsman, intelligent and a very popular.

Dad rarely, if ever, told James or me anything of his earlier life. The change of name organised by Kate Parker was a well kept secret and was never discussed. Just sometimes, he would tell us a little of the past. We knew that our grandfather had been an hotelier and had once managed the Royal Bath Hotel in Bournemouth while his wife Kate, somehow or other, ran a second hotel in Hastings, the Albany, in addition to looking after her eleven children.

I have sometimes wondered why my father was so reticent in talking to us about the past, but thinking about it I am beginning to appreciate how very difficult things must have been for Dad when he was growing up. When the First World War with all its terrible consequences broke out, Eric was just 11 years old and at boarding school. "Schwabe, you are a bloody German!" It is easy to imagine the names he may have been called by other pupils, even if only in jest. And then, just a year or two later, another indignity when at his mother's bidding he changed his name from Schwabe to Parker.

After leaving school Eric joined Imperial Chemical Industries (ICI), one of our country's largest and most successful businesses,

Eric and Kathleen Parker

and so began a marvellous career which lasted for forty years. In some respects ICI was run on service lines with its executives expected to undertake a variety of jobs so as to gain all-round experience of the company. When promoted to a Sales Manager Dad sold a bewildering range of products – dyestuffs, paints, fertilisers, chemicals, plastics, explosives, soda ash, acrylics, with each new product often resulting in a move to another part of England. Throughout his working life Dad would average a move every three years.

In the 1920's during a period when he was working in London, Eric joined the Honourable Artillery Company as a Horseman and once a year he would go to Salisbury Plain for two weeks annual exercises and manoeuvres. "I was considered a poor horseman," he told me, "and always rode the horse nearest to the gun carriage." "How did you manage?' I asked. "Well it was not as difficult as it sounds as providing one could cling on; the horses knew exactly what to do." Many years later I happened to be in London on the Queen Mother's birthday. The Royal horse Artillery with six guns stopped close to where I was standing. I started thinking about Dad.

The Royal Horse Artillery

In 1931 Eric married Kathleen Annie Lees the daughter of a successful hat maker in Manchester, Lancashire. In between the Great Wars Stockport was renowned for its quality hats. If you want to get ahead, get a hat ran the well-known advertising slogan. To this day Stockport's Football Club is known as the 'Hatters'. Sadly the Hatters rarely manage to climb far from the bottom of the league.

Eric James Croft Parker

By extraordinary coincidence Kathleen's elder sister Mary had married Sidney Astle, who in the First World War had fought in the Somme alongside the the Royal Sussex. He was wounded and awarded the Military Cross. In the Second World War he reformed his battalion and spent another four years of his life with the British Army. Sidney and Cecil met at a number of family gatherings, but they never to my knowledge spoke a word about their war. Did Sidney Astle ever know that Cecil and his brother Sidney were both involved in the disastrous battle of Beaumont Hamel where he too had been fighting alongside the 11th Sussex the day it suffered such heavy losses that it ceased to exist as a fighting unit? Perhaps it was too painful a memory to

Sidney Astle

recall or talk about.

Eric and Kathleen's was a good and happy marriage with both partners lovers of sport. They went skating in the winter – I guess it was colder in those days – and our mother was shortlisted for the English Ladies Lacrosse team. In the summer Kathleen played tennis whenever she could while Eric played good club cricket. He too would play tennis or even bowls in the long summer evenings.

I was born in 1933 and James followed four years later. By then the family was already on the move: Mill Hill in North London followed by a house opposite Shenley Aerodrome – an exciting place during the London Blitz where James and I would sometimes look for shrapnel when the all-clear had sounded – and then to Bramhall, Manchester, all in a few months.

From the age of 7, James and I spent the majority of our time at boarding school. Did it do us any harm? Well I am not sure, but it certainly gave us some marvellous opportunities, with James, much to the family's pride, becoming one of the best young cricketers in the land.

Dad was a great host with a wide circle of friends. His other hobbies included golf and horse racing. Without in any way being a true gambler, he liked nothing more than a flutter covering more or less any event. Rumour has it that bets were just as likely to be struck in an ICI Board Room as at Sandown Park Racetrack.

Dad was a perfectionist, everything had to be done correctly and in order, the grapefruit spoons were not to be kept with the teaspoons, and it was important to be polite and courteous at all times. Writing this, it occurs to me that in those ways Eric was very much August's son.

Dad died when he was only sixty eight, he had for most of his life been a heavy smoker, and sadly because of that he died far too young. A good man in every way; James and I still miss him, but I think I speak for both of us, we should have liked to have known him better.

CHAPTER 10
THE SECRET

When I started writing our family history, I wanted to try to find out more about my grandfather, Charles August Schawbe and what his story was. What a journey it has turned out to be. With much help from family members, I have found out so much, not only about August but also about his remarkable wife and children. And what a supporting cast of characters we have – Conan Doyle, Edmund Blunden, and Arthur Ransom to name just three!

I have called our story *A Question of Identity* and it seems to me that so much is tied up in the secret which has haunted our family for so many years.

In 1915 things were going badly, August had died leaving his family with little money and the war was an utter disaster. Kate Parker while grieving for her husband, was angry and embarrassed by the way she and her family were being treated. To be called a 'bloody German' in the street and shunned by others was difficult for her and even worse for her children while the growing casualty lists in the newspapers and tales of German atrocities made for more difficulties. So, for better or worse, Kate decided that the only solution was to change the family name and that the change would be a secret. Kate was strong-minded, determined and wanted a fresh start.

Despite the tribulations of the First World War the family were determined survivors and ten members of the original family were still alive in 1939, including mother Kate, who was still looking after her unmarried daughters. In the meanwhile, a new generation of Parkers were growing with many of them knowing absolutely nothing of what had gone on before.

I wonder if the secret change of name was a help or a hindrance, another burden for her children to carry for the rest of their lives. The First World War left its mark not only on Charles and Cecil but on others too. Charles, able, intelligent and attractive had his demons and left a difficult inheritance for his children. Cecil, a remarkable man, seemed unfazed by his wartime experience and rarely if ever talked about it. I wonder if his daughter Angela knew. Godfrey Parker and Eric Parker who both started out as Schwabes never told their children about their change of name and Kathleen Schwabe only told her daughter Daphne when the Second World War was over. There is little doubt that the secret left its mark on most of us, a secret which was reinforced by the horrors of the Second World War as the Nazis swept through Europe.

As for me, I was a grown man with a family of my own when I found out, quite by chance, that my father had once been a German named Eric James Croft Schwabe.

I was driving to London and had just passed Crawley when I switched on the radio to listen to the news. The BBC was broadcasting a short tribute to the actor Cecil Parker who had just died. The critic said he had been a marvellous actor, but he had a darker side and his real name was Cecil Schwabe. What nonsense, I thought. I had known Cecil all my life, trust the BBC to get it wrong.

The following week I called on my mother and asked her if it was true that Uncle Cecil was in fact somebody else.

"Of course it is," my mother replied, "all you Parkers are Germans."

"Why didn't you tell James and me?" I asked .

"Well there never seemed a right time when we were not fighting the bloody Germans."

My mother came from Manchester. She was a plain speaker.

CHAPTER 11
AUDREY MARY ELIZABETH SCHWABE

Aunt Audrey lived to the age of 84, much longer than any of her ten brothers and sisters. She was the youngest but one of August and Kate's children and was born in 1906, just 8 years before the First World War. When war was declared her three eldest brothers left home to join the British army as front line soldiers, but that did nothing to stop strangers, even neighbours, from shouting abuse at her and her family for being German. It would have been a bewildering and frightening time for Audrey and even worse when in 1915, her father August died from stomach cancer and her mother, Kate, instructed the family to change their name from Schwabe to Parker. I doubt that anyone had the time to love and comfort Audrey in those difficult days.

For many years I saw very little of Audrey – of course there was the occasional family get together, often it seemed for a funeral – but I did call and see Margery, Sally and Audrey when they were living at Bargate in Godalming close to Copse Hanger. The three of them gave me a very warm welcome. Margery was very crippled with her terrible arthritis but in good heart; Sally with her infectious laugh produced some splendid scones and Audrey chatted away seeking news of our family – was James, an exceptional cricketer, making lots of runs and was my mother still playing tennis? Had I seen the cyclamens in Gwen's garden and how was Dennis? It was a good visit.

Then just a few years later Margery and Sally had died and Audrey was living alone. I had some business in Guilford and so from time to time – not as often as I should – I would call and see Audrey on my way home to Brighton. Despite being ill and frail, Audrey was brave and determined – she would do her best to face anything that life might throw at her. Audrey's real pleasure in her last years was to talk and receive news about her family and was more interested in the future than the past. "Daf is coming tomorrow and I hope she will bring Katherine with her; it will be good to see them. Have you met any of Judy's children? What about Julian is he still at sea, and have you seen, Sara's market garden, it is quite something." Well I did call and see Sara's market garden – Audrey was right.

It was during one of my infrequent visits that Audrey gave me her father and my grandfather, August Schwabe's, signet ring and his marvellous paper knife. She explained that as I had become the oldest male member of the Parker Schwabe family that it was my duty to look after the two precious items. It was an emotional moment and just a few months later Audrey died. Audrey was the last of the Parker Schawbes, but our family and her legacy continues. Time marches on, and so I am passing the signet ring down the line to Julian and the paper knife to James. I wish all our large and remarkable family the very best for the future. Who will write the next chapter?

As I sit here now, re-reading our family story, I realise that it has been Audrey, old and alone but with a deep love of our family, who has been the inspiration behind our efforts. Equal thanks are due to Katherine, Daphne and Dick's elder daughter who brought the family together and told us who we were.

Love and best wishes to all
Tim Parker
January 2017